SEA OF TRANQUILITY
A LITERARY ANTHOLOGY

South Florida Writers Association Authors
Lunar Codex

SEA OF TRANQUILITY
A LITERARY ANTHOLOGY

South Florida Writers Association Authors
Lunar Codex

Copyright © 2024 South Florida Writers Association
First Edition

Edited by the Sea of Tranquility Team
Published by the South Florida Writers Association (SFWA)
in the USA
Cover Art by Regine Fisher
Cover and formatting by SusanasBooks, LLC.

South Florida Writers Association
P.O. Box 56-2652
Miami, FL 33256

https://www.southfloridawriters.org/
https://x.com/WritersSouth
https://www.instagram.com/southfloridawriters/
https://www.facebook.com/SFWAConnection/
https://www.youtube.com/channel/UCcl-Zf1T5TsDZTJtvPyb1Pg

All rights reserved. Except for brief excerpts in reviews, no part of this book may be transmitted in any form or by any means, electronic or physical, including photocopying, recording, in any information storage or retrieval system, in part, or any form, without the authors' permission. Individual authors retain the right to republish their work.

Paperback ISBN: 978-0-9960369-5-5

For the trailblazers, the pioneers, and the wanderers of wonder. For those who reach for that space between stars and touch majesty.

We are forever grateful.

TABLE OF CONTENTS

Cover Art by Regine Fisher

Preface Mare Tranquillitatis—Samuel Peralta.................... viii

Introduction—Howard Camner x

Launched—Jonathan Rose.. 1

Lunar Codex (artwork)—Cathy Lowen 2

A Lunar Conversation—C.V. Shaw...................................... 3

A Moon Filled Night On Distant Shore—Mark Bonaparte 5

A Silvery Snow Moon—Barbra Nightingale............................ 7

Astronauts And The Celestial Lunar Light—Linda M. Campbell...... 8

Celestial Anomaly—Cynthia Uzzolino.................................10

Does the U.S. Have A Moon Too—Dale Alan Young....................11

Eleanor Kleiner Uncovers the Moon—Brian Shaer 12

Eternal Echo—Mark Lew...13

Flight by Night—Jen Karetnick...16

For a Sleepless Child—Peter Schmitt...................................19

Celestial Wonders (artwork)—Keiana Morgan 20

Foil—Lenny DellaRocca..21

Friendly Moon—Jo Avent 22

Full Moon And Love—Joanne Sherry Mitchell 24

Full Moon Haiku—Mary Greenwood.....................................25

Gray Moon—Mikaelo Perez...26

LIGHT QUEEN…the Moon—Raining Deer aka Jeanette Stephens-El..28

Luna— C.V. Shaw...30

Luna over Akrotiri— Susana Jiménez-Mueller 31

Lunar Experience—Ricki Dorn 34

Lunar Whisperings—Jonathan Rose 35

Midnight Dream—Connie Goodman-Milone 38

Moon Dreams—Carla Albano 39

Robot World (artwork)—Richard Frost 41

Moondance: Moon, Sun and Earth Canticles—Gail S. Tucker-Griffith 42

Moonlight and Roses—Carolyn McBride 43

Moonlight On A Lonely Night—Joanne Sherry Mitchell 45

My Twelve Moons—Cara Nusinov 46

New Moon—Swati Bagga 48

On A Winter Night—Geoffrey Philp 50

Phases—Charles Maxim Bernstein 51

Phases of the Moon—Cynthia Uzzolinol 53

Poetry in Porcelain—Mort Laitner 54

Same Moon—Anita Mitchell 57

Strawberry Super Moon—Barbra Nightingale 59

Amy (artwork)—Richard Frost 61

The Lunar Library—Beverly Melasi-Haag 62

The Lunar Beasts—Giancarlo Diago Cevallos 66

The Man In The Moon, For Real—Howard Camner 69

The Moon—Fabiyas M V 71

The Moon And I Walk The Dog—Neil Crabtree 72

The Moon Changing Me—Billy Jones 74

The Moon: Fear, Science, and Love—Gladys A. Barrio 76

The Moon Obscured—Howard Camner *81*

Phases (artwork)—Charles Maxim Bernstein *83*

The Neglected Moon after Baudelaire —Steve Kronen *84*

To The Moon In Joy—Christina Moss Mayo *85*

Tokyo Games 2020—Connie Goodman-Milone *88*

Trashing the Moon and Mars—Pat Bonner Milone *89*

Waning Crescent—Pat Bonner Milone *91*

What Does the Moon Mean to Me—Monica DeZulueta *92*

Winter Moon—Geoffrey Philp *94*

Wishes Under the Full Moon—Meg Nocero *97*

Dolly Attacks (artwork)—Richard Frost *99*

Lunar Codex Party Planning Is Hard—Mort Laitner *100*

Epilogue—Mort Laitner *103*

About the Authors *105*

vii

PREFACE
MARE TRANQUILLITATIS

On Earth's Moon, early astronomers saw through their telescopes what they imagined were seas, or *maria* in Latin. One of the largest – at about 876 kilometers in diameter, or roughly 544 miles – they named *Mare Tranquillitatis*, the Sea of Tranquility.

In truth, these were not seas at all but large basaltic plains, formed by ancient lava flows into basins formed by the impact of other celestial bodies like meteors on the Moon's surface.

On July 20, 1969, just over 55 years ago, the Sea of Tranquility became the site for the first crewed landing on the Moon, when the Apollo 11 lunar module *Eagle* made a successful descent.

It was a dream made real. On landing, astronauts Neil Armstrong and Buzz Aldrin radioed back to Earth the message: "Houston, *Tranquility Base* here. The *Eagle* has landed."

Fifty-five years later, this book – the *Sea of Tranquility* anthology – has been commissioned for the *Lunar Codex* project. Launching in one of its missions to the Moon, it brings together the voices of scores of poets and authors in commemoration of that first Moon landing.

It is a tribute to the spirit of humanity – whether astronomer, astronaut, or poet – and its yearnings, to look upward, outward, to imagine, to dream. And to make it real.

Samuel Peralta
Founder, The Lunar Codex

Toronto, Canada
August 2024

INTRODUCTION

"I like to think that the moon is there, even if I am not looking at it."

Albert Einstein

The Lunar Codex is a one-of-a-kind phenomenon. There has never been anything like it. The New York Times calls it "A time capsule of human creativity stored in the sky" because that's what it is, the works of some 35,000 contemporary artists, writers, poets, musicians and filmmakers from 253 countries, territories and indigenous nations on planet Earth. Those creations are rocketed to the moon for a three day journey of 238,900 miles in time capsules that will remain as a permanent footprint; a gifted archive from one planet to another. For those artists included in this historic event it is immortality, in a very real sense. At a time of great division on planet Earth, it is the artists who rise above, unify, and make the impossible happen.

The Lunar Codex is the brainchild of Dr. Samuel Peralta: renowned physicist, artist, art curator, filmmaker, poet and excellent chef! Sam wears many hats. Me, I wear one. It's the beat-up fedora of a street poet who has seen a thing or two. I've worn it for half a century behind more microphones than I could count, sending my characters with all their idiosyncrasies out into the world to make their way. I was involved in the Lunar Codex long before I even knew it. To be honest, I can't remember how I found out. Several issues of Poets & Artists

Arts Journal that included my poetry was set to go to the moon. Its publisher, Didi Menendez, was a longtime friend who had published me both as a solo poet and in collaboration issues with some amazing visual artists. Didi had also published a poetry book for a visionary physicist named Samuel Peralta. Sam and I connected and became friends as well. When there was a delay in a launch, Sam asked me to create an anthology of poetry and flash fiction handing me the reins and telling me to bring in whoever I wanted to be included in the Codex. The anthology (along with my other work) would be included in the last of the Lunar Codex missions: the Polaris. Previous missions include Orion, Peregrine, Nova, Serenity, Minerva and Freya.

Of all of them, Polaris would be paramount because it contains the entire global Lunar Codex. I knew I would need help putting the anthology together and contacted the president of the South Florida Writers Association, Mort Laitner, who I knew could get things rolling, as Sam had given me a deadline to get the anthology to him. If you're reading this, mission accomplished.

This anthology includes the work of SFWA members, other poets I have worked with creatively throughout the years, and "The Old Guard".

The Old Guard, as I call "us", are a small group of Miami's original "stable of bards" that gathered and performed at

Miami's premier bookstore "Books & Books" when it first opened in 1982 with the turn of proprietor and literary activist Mitchell Kaplan's key. As I write this, that was 42 years ago. Together we helped put "the cultural desert that was Miami" on the map of the literary world. Now, to the moon we go. I wish to thank Mort for his invaluable help. This anthology could not have...gotten off the ground (yes, I know)...without him. I also want to thank our assistant editors and compilers, Monica DeZulueta, Neil Crabtree, and Travis Laitner and everyone involved in putting this project together; all the poets and authors, Amy Nicole Naim, the Sea of Tranquility Public Relations, and of course, the man with vision who made the impossible possible, Dr. Samuel Peralta—So onward (and upward).

Howard Camner - Miami, Florida - August 3rd, 2024

Launched

A LUNAR CODEX on the moon,

Threescore and six years--not too soon--

To recognize an amazing time

And renew the spirit of sixty-nine!

Jonathan Rose, Miami Beach, Miami-Dade County, Florida

Lunar Codex

Cathy Lowen, Bellevue, King County, Washington

A Lunar Conversation

I sit here lotus position

Jeweled up in beads

Drinking warm teas made of strange weeds

Trying to elevate from this physical plane

I'm comfortable where they think me insane

I inhale deep breathes to take it all in

Trying to detach from the artificial world I live in

I gaze at the stars

I gaze at the moon

Further I travel

I'll be up there soon

Where the celestial bodies look down and smile

Taking pity on humans with their materialistic style

"If only they knew," I can hear them say

"The peace they would find if they'd just change their way"

"A million years more," the moon dares to speak

"Their fears are too strong... their beliefs are too weak"

The stars turn to listen as the moon speaks her mind

"In a million years more, perhaps faith they'll find"

"What can we do," the stars turn to say

The moon spins around, "keep lighting their way"

Little by little I start floating down

Cars buzzing by

Radios blaring

People cursing and people staring

I look at the moon and I swear it smiles

The stars twinkle at me across the miles

I reach my hands up and grab their magic to borrow

I wink at the sky and whisper

"I'll be back tomorrow"

C.V. Shaw, Miami, Miami - Dade County, Florida

A Moon Filled Night on Distant Shore

A moon filled night I strolled along,
deep thoughts I pondered.
How magnificent the Universe,
how shallow I had wandered.

That marbled orb of iridescence
that a myriad mysteries inspires
prompted me to introspect
and question my desires.

What held me here on distant shore
far from my true desire?
Was I fearful of that place
or lacked the inner fire?

T'was not what I comprehended
that captivated me,
rather stirrings in my soul.
Who did I want to be?

Most elusive and intimate
that which I long did seek
was my own other being
that within me speaks.
The ghostly, shimmering moonbeam

that hovered beyond my grasp
turned the darkest of bleakness
to a silvery, shining path.

A moon filled night on distant shore,
no more deep thoughts I ponder.
I've learned to let my music play.
No longer need I wander.

Mark Bonaparte, Miami, Miami-Dade County, Florida

A Silvery Snow Moon

is beautiful, I'm sure, somewhere
up north where the cold earns its name,
where the sparkles flicker on the ice,
the hard pack glinting in the yard.

In February, chances are the melt
has not yet begun, the quiet insulation
still buffeting city sounds,
bouncing off the drifts.

Here, under the same-named moon,
grey rain and humid skies,
the hum of my air conditioner
muffles my neighbor's dog.

Down here in Paradise, where we debate
the sea's rising, the day's rise and fall,
what children can say to their teachers.
But the moon? It turns its face,
going once around the sun.
The same as earth.

Barbra Nightingale, Hollywood, Broward County, Florida

Astronauts and the Celestial Lunar Light

Lunar modules race to the moon carrying astronauts to explore, thinking of returning, evermore. And the allure of the spaceship headed to the moon will be astounding and deliriously appealing for many very soon. Are we ready to take this trip many say, and the answer is often, yesterday! Ah, how sweet the trip to the lunar moon. How awesome the adventure coming very soon.

The enthusiastic astronauts eagerly await their impending flight to expectingly capture a whimsical glimpse of stars at night, glistening and glowing in atmospheric delight. Soon to evolve and ascend above earth's surface, astronauts eagerly await the spectacular lunar sight, the moon always magnificent in its own rite. While on earth, observers will soon canonize the modular flight.

How often the moon in its lunar wonderland evades the simplistic understanding of man; yet, the stars communicate with it on a lunar galactical plane. As stars descend and ascend the ladder of space, the moon in its glory stands in its official place. A place in the universe designed by God to light the sky by night; then, move aside by day to give way to sunlight.

How magnificent is the moon's shining lunar light of night, adorned in its finery for earth's delight.

We adore the moon and its beauty and rest in its light, as astronauts soon ascend into the heavens to explore such a grand and spectacular site.

Linda M. Campbell, Aventura, Miami-Dade County, Florida

Celestial Anomaly

A selenophile, I am - lover of the moon

my name, of Greek origin means - goddess of the moon

star seed child, I am

stretching my soul out into the universe to find home

the spent wishes on balls of gas burning too far away

float around like space debris in the stratosphere

but there it orbits like an angel on its guard

theorized to have been an anomaly from Earth's collision with

Theia

this celestial beauty waxing and waning through our days

its cratered, pockmarked surface

highlands, maria and sea of tranquility

all viewable to the naked eye

the closest thing to heaven I will ever see

the love story I wished for I now find underneath its fullness

its magnetism pulls me in as it does the oceans' tide

willing me to come back home.

Cynthia Uzzolino, Miramar, Broward County, Florida

Does the U.S. Have a Moon Too?

"Hoy, otro viaje a la luna," shouted
The newspaper boy on a Bogotá street corner
as I passed by.
The boy asked me to translate the headline.
"Today, another moon landing."
I explained that US astronauts
Walked on the moon today.
He looked bewildered.
"Does the United States have a moon too?"
His perspective blew me away.
Why are US astronauts walking on Colombia's moon?
Does his moon belong to Colombia?
Does that mean that the big dipper belonged
To the African slaves who followed it north to freedom?
Does the North Star belong to Canada?
If Argentina claims the Southern Cross,
Will Chile dispute it?
Does Orion belong to the Greeks because they named it?
Is it like the children's game *Finder's Keepers*?
"I saw it first, so it's mine." Or
Are these vestiges of colonialism?
We landed on it. We planted our country's flag.
It's our moon.

Dale Alan Young, Miami, Miami-Dade County, Florida

Eleanor Kleiner Uncovers the Moon

Oh, Eleanor, Eleanor, such magnificent light.

Looking up to the sky, at stars beaming bright.

Cosmic wonders of number; Big Dipper, North Star.

Forces one to realize how insignificant they are.

On such a clear night, so much luminescence.

It appears the sky is bathed in fluorescence.

The occasional jet glides through velvety dark.

Its flickers of red and flickers of white bestow to the quiet a

sporadic spark.

But a thick slice of white, such brilliant radiation.

So much so, Eleanor, to divert your attention.

It knows that its charms cannot be forsaken.

You can't pull away, not for TV nor bacon.

Its ethereal sway draws out peace and reflection.

Begging you, Eleanor, to accept its connection.

Ancient moon, in the ether, kiss me goodnight.

Oh, Eleanor, Eleanor, such magnificent light.

Brian Shaer, Wilton Manors, Broward County, Florida

Eternal Echo

"Really?! The best you can come up with is a comedy?"

"And what's wrong with coming up with something funny, huh?"

She rolled her eyes at me. "First off, you're not that funny."

Nodding, I answered, "That may be, but the bar is set really low. I mean, how many people are sending a lighthearted piece of humor up to the moon? I don't actually need to be funny... just funnier! And with zero competition, I—"

"And you want *that* to be your contribution to posterity?"

"Hey! Laughter is what makes life worth living! Besides, it's not like anyone is actually going to read the stuff! I hate to break it to you, but there aren't any *Moonies* living there."

"You can't know that for certain," she said, smirking.

"Okay... maybe I can't; I'll give you that. But I can say with certainty they have a less-than-zero chance of being able to read English, so they won't understand it anyway."

"So, you think laughter trumps love, compassion, and empathy as the thing that makes life worth living?!"

Uh oh... I saw the minefield she'd just laid, knowing I had a pretty good shot at blowing myself up. If I said "no" too quickly, she'd see right through it, but if I said "yes" then she'd wonder how she could have married such a shallow man and let doubts start to trickle in. I had to think fast, skirt the territory entirely.

"Wanna hear a joke?" I asked.

"No… not really. Not now. I want you to answer my question."

"Three men walk into a bar, a man whose heart was filled with compassion, one whose love for humanity knew no bounds, and a comedian."

"I said, *no,*" she objected.

"So the bartender asks the first one what he could get him."

Her soft expression hardened to a glare. I knew why, but crossing the minefield was my only other choice.

"A round for everyone!" he said, as everyone cheered.

Next, the bartender asked the second one what he wanted.

"Whatever it is, put your best effort into it and I'll love it."

Then, the bartender asked the third man what he wanted.

"Nothing. I don't drink."

"So, what're you doing in a bar?"

"Trying to teach my wife a lesson."

She tried hard not to laugh, pursed her lips as tightly as she could, but it burst out of her throat with unbridled force (and a little spittle, I might add) as she tried to contain herself.

So it is not my joke that's being left as my legacy; it's the echo of her laughter floating through eternity.

Mark Lew, Hollywood, Broward County, Florida

Flight by Night

A golden shovel after Rush, for transport on the Codex Polaris

Named for the season's rampant ripening, this year's
Strawberry Moon
peaked during summer solstice for the first time in forty years.
I watched it rise,

sipping the berry-studded sangria on which the most
enterprising, thoughtful
beach bar promoters capitalized. On the moon-blazed sand
around me, other eyes

gazed through cellphone lenses, augmented by filters, flashes,
egos. Rosy orb staring
in the background, they clicked selfies for social media they'd
never thumb back

through again. Earlier, I read the Old Farmer's Almanac. For
all the month of June, at
places like Fairbanks and Reykjavik, the moon wouldn't even
knock at the horizon. For me,

from where I stood on unceded Algonquian land, where
months were logged from
Sap to Sturgeon, depending on the harvest, a Moon Illusion
summited at 9 pm as the

lowest and appear as the biggest, with the same reflectance of
asphalt. A tinted window,
the moon shows what bounces off its surface, as if the core—
or the science—is beside

the point. This near-Earth object, our only natural satellite, is
just a rock, after all. No
need to remind onlookers that the moon drifts away by
centimeters each year, cause fright

that the ancient collective unconscious can't handle. No call to
mention moonquakes or
the tides of movement it pulls not just in water but also in the
dirt of bodies. Hindsight

tells us that a Mars-sized object crashed into Earth 4.5 billion
years ago, leaving
us this mystical, lunar pebble, 400 times smaller than the sun.
1.3 light-seconds behind,

I looked up at this moonprojecting fire, creating at least one
more human that
wants to land on it, plant a country's flag, find out where there
is water, and empty
our mortal problems on it. An astrologer told me my moon
sign forecasted the opposite feeling.

A bit burnt out, he said. Rest and recharge. I disagreed until
tines of lightning drove me inside.

Jen Karetnick, El Portal, Miami-Dade County, Florida

For a Sleepless Child

If your room is ever too dark,
small one, look out through your window
up at the moon, that little bulb
left on for you in the sky's black wall.
It will still be there come morning,
burning in a bright room of blue.

And if your room, restless one,
is much too still, listen to the clatter
of the freight, rattling past trestles
on the cool night breeze. Then follow
the moon to the side of the tracks,
where the train is a long, slow dream

you can jump on. An open car
is waiting for you—one step up—
you're on! Now watch the dark towns, the lights
deep in the porches, and lie down
in the soft straw, and sleep till morning,
when the train chugs into the station,
noisy with birds and wires overhead.

Peter Schmitt, Miami, Miami-Dade County, Florida

Celestial Wonders

Keiana Morgan, San Jose, Santa Clara County, California

Foil

Foil keeps gravity sane though I'm still a balloon on one side of a see-saw. Shoes wrapped in foil keeps out spiders. Spiders get big ideas in shoes. I sit quietly and foil sad-faced afternoons whose beautiful after-masturbation sighs become clouds in a pop song. Yes, that one. The moon goes around the sky in a goofy loop-d-loop so I wrap it up good and shiny. It's to it keep what little gravity it has close to its heart. Aluminum foil keeps medicine's side-effects away: cramps, poems about awful things, walls that close in, and language that can't get past The, a, the, a, the, a. Anne Sexton says Nine clocks spring open and smash themselves against the sun. I Grok that. So I wrap my cock in foil, which is why time erases life click by click, why my breath is foggy when my watch stops cold. Did I say cock. Sorry, clock. Anne says The calendars of the world burn if you touch them. So I wrap the months in foil in case they're haunted by fire. Pretty sure they are. I see January ghosts in sunsets, February's at midnights. You get the idea. By the way, foil and desire are like oil and vinegar.

Try jacking off with a fistful of foil. I've found out why some folks wear foil cones on their heads. It's not to block signals from the CIA or aliens from outer space. Don't be ridiculous. It's to disrupt their mother's anti-gravity ray, to keep their godforsaken feet on the ground.

Lenny DellaRocca, Delray Beach, Palm Beach County, Florida

Friendly Moon

Consider our knife-edge dance through life on earth

As easily as a snapped twig we can be broken,

As quickly as a candle extinguished

Deaths, fast and slow come to both young and old

We rise in fortune and lose it all

We win in love and then are bereft

How to make sense of the chutes and ladders of life?

Surely, it will take a comfort from beyond our world

Cloud ensconced gods can not be relied upon

For they have their own agendas

Let's turn our attention further into the skies to find comfort

Seeking that peace in an eternal rhythm

The heartbeats felt in our mother's womb

Some look eastwards

They wait for him to appear and stride across the sky

He follows the same path, steadfast

Always heat and always light

He is a big star, we are not to look directly at him

He is nuclear, he can support growth and he can destroy

He can give life

He can give death

He is a double-edged sword
Still we are fans; we revolve around him
I however, wait for you

You generously share your stage and allow others to shine
Revealing to explorers inklings in inky skies and bestowing
romance on lovers
Ancient stories play out on your Seurat canvas
Formed of us, you encircle us, you travel with us
Your gentle rhythms match those of my own
The oceans rise and fall as a rocked cradle
Your shape waxing and waning, soft echo of the tides
You grow from blackness to gravid fullness
And how you glow!
Remarked on through car windows and across cityscapes and
meadows alike
Oh friendly face, void of judgement
Who hasn't felt less alone when you are there?
Then, ebbing nightly you diminish to nothing
We learn to trust that you will return
We grasp that we too can take different forms
We understand that some experiences are a phase
We know we have a friend out there

Jo Avent, Pinecrest, Miami-Dade County, Florida

Full Moon and Love

Love by the Full Moon

There is not a scene that excites me more

Than watching the Full Moon

Rise from the sea

Large enough to imagine it's a monster

Coming to visit

We kiss until our lips are swollen

With a few mosquitos and their bits

When completed with our love secession

We watch the entire show given

To us by the

Full Moon rise

We say our good nights for

The night is over

Now its morning

I know

The Full Moon will rise again

In 29 and 1/4 days

What i do not know

Will my girlfriend be mine in

29 and 1/4 days

Joanne Sherry Mitchell, Coral Gables, Miami-Dade County, Florida

Full Moon Haiku

Sun and Moon aligned,

Moon cannot shine its own light.

The Moon reflects the sun.

Mary Greenwood, Dunedin, Pinellas County, Florida

Gray Moon

Moon, why are you gray?

Was it the asteroids, crash landing and denting your body?

Was it the comets, racing past and never greeting?

Was it the sun, leaving you in darkness?

Was it man, choosing to sleep in your wake?

Are you lonely?

Moon, are you gray?

As a boy, I asked myself these questions, and forgive me for my inattention. I've seen you sanguine donning crimson blush, I've seen you blackened by an inky brush.

I've seen you pallid after a blinding dawn— I see you blue, once in a blue moon.

And forgive me for my inattention, for I am unable to see both sides of your

face when it wanes. An iron coin that I can only choose heads or tails of, yet either prospect is lucky.

Moon, you are gray and, I personally believe, that it is okay. Reflected by the ripples on your exterior, I get to peer at your heart. Inside you I see the light that guides the owls out and makes the canines howl. Inside I see the silver shine that ricochets off of stars when they scintillate. From inside, I can tell, that, gray as you are, you command the ebb of receding waves to ease the journey of the hatchlings down below.

Gray Moon, thank you.

You are beautiful, even if you must weep a little, or if you must
weep for a year.

Every day you come out at night, despite your grayness.

Color does not evade you, instead, it emanates

from you like a glass prism devoid of light itself still incessantly
showering others in it.

You work hard.

Gray Moon, thank you.

Mikaelo Perez, Miami, Miami-Dade County, Florida

LIGHT QUEEN ... the Moon

Royal Moon.

Light Queen of the midnight sky.

Luna.

White knight illuminating

The waters for seafarers

Seeking a golden shore.

Opaque sphere encircling the Sun God

With star beings.

A speck in the pantheon of celestial bodies

That give us pause.

Ma-maw Moon.

Sky angel who watches over

Her earthly children as they

Busy themselves with life,

Unaware of their ever-present protector.

Tide conductor.

Maestra whose mere presence --

In phases – directs the rise and fall

Of the ocean's waking waters.

Wash over us with your brilliance.

Heal us with your medicine.

Bathe us in your milk.

Guide us with your wisdom.

Empower us with your spirit.

Make us eternal with your love light.

Great Sky Warrior Queen.

Diamond of the heavens.

Raining Deer aka Jeanette Stephens-El, Miami, Miami-Dade County, Florida

Luna

Admiring eyes on me tonight

as I reflect over you, the sun's glorious light

I pull on your waters

with my magnetic might

Billions of years

my existence undenied

I shape your home's curves

keeping its wobble precise

Your climate I balance

Your mood I may blight

Provide you four seasons

as I watch in delight

Victorious for your long days

I bask in the night

Watch me as I wane

'til only a sliver of me in sight

C.V. Shaw, Miami, Miami-Dade County, Florida

Luna over Akrotiri

"You are my Luna." Whispered the girl, unfolding her arms as though this very act could engulf the moon in an embrace.

The sun had just dropped behind the line of olive trees, and its last rays lingered on her hair, pulling a myriad of tiny golden sparks into the coolness of the evening. Her face tilted toward the sky, waiting for the perfect moment when her moon would appear – translucent.

It was the year 1546 BCE in the town of Akrotiri, overlooking the prehistoric Aegean Sea. Ever the romantic, Eleni sat crossed-legged on the flat roof, daydreaming, waiting for her Luna—the same unchanging moon who had brought her peace these past few days when the earth rumbled incessantly.

Despite the community's uncertainty, her world was full of magical tales brought to their shores by mariners. Tales of the Chakora, the legendary bird who held the moon close to her heart and fed on its silvery beams. Or the raven, another bird who wanted light and had rolled a boulder off a mountain and put the moon in the sky. Eleni had also heard about an animal called a wolf, who howled at the full moon to express his unrequited love.

She gasped as a shiver traveled up her back when the breeze from the sea picked up, lifting her blue tunic.

The girl held her braided hair close to her neck as she ululated. Her howl, which began as a whimper, emerged fully when darkness swallowed her surroundings, except for the stars above.

The world around her disappeared for a moment, and she imagined herself dancing on that same silvery beam in compass to the stars.

Below her, families prepared to evacuate their homes. And the girl knew, somewhere in the recesses of her mind, that her special place on the roof would be no more. Regardless, Luna, her friend and confidant, would remain her constant.

Eleni heard her father's raspy voice calling her name. She responded, blew Luna a kiss, and slowly descended the wooden ladder to join her family. That night, the north winds would take them to Crete or Egypt, the land of Pharaohs.

Soon, Eleni and her family boarded the longboat. The earth shook, and the sea responded in kind. The darkness of night became day when the volcano erupted violently in what would later be known as the largest eruption in human history—the Minoan eruption, also known as the eruption of Thera.

The ship and its passengers were thrown onto the deck, gasping for air as the two sails unfurled and snapped, catching the thermal wave emanating from the eruption.

Eleni clung to her brother and searched the sky for Luna, but the cloud of ash obscured the moon.

Plastered to the deck, the families didn't witness the sea claiming part of their world. The ship took flight, rising higher and higher—not just riding the thermal, like the wings of a bird, but the wave, which became a tsunami that destroyed nearby islands.

Eleni, still holding her brother tight, softly howled at the moon—and the world went silent.

Susana Jiménez-Mueller, Brandon, Hillsborough County, Florida

Lunar Experience

Moon beams,

Moon dreams,

Journey to a lunar spot

In streams.

Moon shine,

Selenic wine.

Are they cool or are they hot,

those beams?

The man in the moon

Comes to us on Zoom.

His impact will never rot;

It forever gleams.

Moonstone can heal.

Its balance, love, and energy are real.

It is a polyglot.

Many languages it deems.

Ricki Dorn, Miami, Miami-Dade County, Florida

Lunar Whisperings

I used to understand
the whisperings of
asparagus and
Brussels sprouts,
back in my early teens
when I was a philosopher
and a vegetarian.

I was one with vegetables.
Not with carrots.
At least not with cooked carrots.
No, cooked carrots did not speak to me,
nor cauliflower, nor radishes and squash.
My friends were the green vegetables,
the ones that mothers push,
yet more exotic ones at that:
Brussels sprouts, asparagus, and lima beans
(named for the capital of Peru but
pronounced like the Ohio town).
I still wonder . . .
never a peep from the peas.
And I adored peas!

My mother's Canadian cousin
made his fortune in Brussels sprouts--

permanent immigrants from fields in Mexico.

I remember travels to Toronto to visit

during the time vegetables were speaking to me.

(I also recall that they only spoke to me at night

by the light of the moon.)

Vegetables were my confidants.

They would whisper poetry in Spanish;

their favorite poet was Neruda.

Here was my Twilight Zone experience:

the nighttime whisperings predated my knowledge

of my mother's cousin's farms,

and of Neruda's poems.

Stranger still, I had only begun

learning Spanish,

yet I recall understanding

every whispered word.

Vegetables no longer speak to me--

perhaps because of chemicals which coat them,

perhaps due to ozone's porous layer.

All I know is at night I wait,

I listen,

I strain,

yet hear nothing.

No. I listen,

I strain.

I hear

their silence.

Jonathan Rose, Miami Beach, Miami-Dade County, Florida

Midnight Dream

Dipping into these stars
to fill a vast splendor
of velveteen sky, the
reminiscent moon
quietly calls out
for you.

Connie Goodman-Milone, Miami, Miami-Dade County, Florida

Moon Dreams

1969

Before a black and white TV,
Mom gathered us 3,
We felt stranded,
As Apollo 11 landed.

Then a puffy man,
Walked on the moon land,
Mom cried, we stared,
My siblings too young to care.

He planted a flag which waved,
I tucked into my memory cave,
Indelibly stored,
To be forever adored.

1980

As I grew and schooled,
I came to conclude,
That I wanted to be,
A part of space history.

That day came so soon,
As recruiters swooned,
During a frenzied boom,

In exploring space and the moon.

My first job would be,
At a top secret company,
Which toiled in space,
At a breakneck pace.

1986
We built top secret machines,
Shared space travel dreams,
It all ended too soon,
With Shuttle Challengers' doom.

2024
Deep in my memory cave,
Is still engraved,
A vision of a puffy man,
Surrounded by the moon, and cyan.

Carla Albano, Hollywood, Broward County, Florida

Robot World

Richard Frost, West Hollywood, Los Angeles County, California

Moondance: Moon, Sun and Earth Canticles

Moon waxes and wanes

Made Bright by fiery sun

Hidden by its mother earth

Sun's light forms moonlight

Moonlight penetrates tree boughs

Earth's windblown breath gives them life

Morning comes, turns night to day

Moon glows, rimmed in red

Water of life refracting

Cratered face smiles brightly down

Gail S. Tucker-Griffith, North Miami, Miami-Dade County, Florida

Moonlight and Roses

Many moons ago, there was a life before him and a moonlit path of promise. Shoot for the moon, they said, when I graduated from high school. And so I went after my dreams, moonlighting to make my way through college. Ask for the moon, they said, when I entered the work force. And so I landed a corporate job and started making my way up the career ladder.

Our paths crossed under a moonbeam at the neighborhood lake. When he freed my dog entangled in a rose bush, I was sure he hung the moon. On our first date, we shared a moon pie, and soon I was moonstruck, drunk on the moonshine in his veins, caught in his gravitational pull like an incoming tide. When he got down on one knee and promised the moon, I was over the moon, nearly moonwalking on air.

With moon-eyed optimism, we wished on a full moon for a life of love and laughter. A miracle happened on our honeymoon and, before long, I was singing "the cow jumped over the moon" to our moon-faced baby boy. We loved him to the moon and back, and the three of us reached for the moon together as many a moon rose and set over the milestones in our life.

Shoot for the moon, we told that baby when he graduated from high school. Ask for the moon, we counseled as he made his way in the world. We were over the moon when he met his own moonbeam, even paid for their honeymoon. And a few years later, the cow jumped over the moon again when we welcomed our first grandchild.

Year in and year out we lived and loved under the same moon. But every full moon must set. They told me his medical condition happened once in a blue moon. If only I could have missed that moon. Without him, I was on the dark side of the moon, his light extinguished. How many moons would I have to go on without him?

My hair is now a pearly moonstone, my eyes barely able to see the man in the moon as I wait for my moonset. I look up and wonder if he's looking down at me, maybe from the far side of the moon, remembering our journey around the moon together that started with moonlight and roses.

Carolyn McBride, Hypoluxo, Palm Beach County, Florida

Moonlight on a Lonely Night

Moon Goddess

Sparkles a plenty

Shines through the grand oak tree

Right into my window

I lay in bed

Watching her rise

While she shines light

On my bed

Moon Goddess whispers to me

Why are you alone tonight

There is no way to answer

The hurt of lonely arises

From the pit of my stomach

Which I held down with great skill

Melancholy hits as I watch

The magic of nature

Wanting the

Magic of love

By moonlight

Joanne Sherry Mitchell, Coral Gables, Miami-Dade County, Florida

My Twelve Moons

Ya better watch out or you may get hooked

by a fisherman or by a view out here,

where pelicans fly right by your nose,

eyewitnesses wander on the wharf over the waves,

waiting. Dusk arrives, enfolding the cumulus vista,

creating jeweled rivers, facets, and sunset sky streams.

We wait. We look to the horizon and predict. *Where?*

Some pray or hope. Wonder. *Will it be hidden this time?*

It's a monthly rite, this anticipation and then, *Oh, it's there.*

The fisherman, my new friend, points.

Luna, he whispers, and the ruby slice peeks through,

emerges, rises by degrees between two clouds,

a van Gogh painting. Pink Moon, Beaver Moon, Buck Moon,

Cold moon.

And every once in a while, a Blue Moon. Twelve full moons.

An assembly awed. Cameras clicks, cell phones witness, people

point, stare,

passionate about moonrise, forgetting constant chaos here on

earth.

Each month another party. Twelve times a year we gather

and I hold my breath like a child waiting for ice cream.

A little boy asks, *Daddy will I see the footprints?* and raises his binoculars again. This month, the Pink Moon.

I see refracted light, though deep in my cells, one part of my
being
thinks it's magic, or the gods. My constant companion, my
celestial torch,
my Dione, I adore you, with all your craters, your ice plains,
and scared terrains,
I am smitten. When it's my time to die, I'll fly to the moon,
leave a forever footprint.

Cara Nusinov, Lake Worth, Palm Beach County, Florida

New Moon

In the bright blue sky
I saw you at first
Just a smudge of a cloud
My apologies Dear Moon

You looked so lost
In the vastness of the sky
Only an outline of a crescent
And Forgive me for I laughed

At the insipid dysfunctional
just a speck of a moon
And I have known you through time
With the silver serenity blanketed world

And the glistening palm at night
the glittering bobbing waves
The Night Queen's sweet lingering fragrance
As it blooms only when you walk the skies

I have known you dearly
In the pure white chilly nights
When bare feet traced tiny steps
On the cold terrace marble
When Maa placed in your gracious presence

Special *Kheer* in a fine muslin covered pot
with the loving faith of divine *Amrut* drops
Gently falling during your brilliant September full bloom

I know you from the countless stories
Shared searching the pearly night sky
Lying In the dreamy net canopy
beneath the heavenly skies

Secured falling asleep as my little fingers traced
twinkling stars in the cold desert night
A zealous wonder at simple things
Tranquil in your presence even when unseen

Anchored countless years of good living
Now Coming full circle to untold stories
As you hold testimony
I know now losing is the cleansing-a new rebirth Dear Moon

Swati Bagga, Miami, Miami-Dade County, Florida

On a Winter Night

On a winter night

when you look up at the moon

know I am with you

Geoffrey Philp, North Miami Beach, Miami-Dade County, Florida

Phases

new moon waiting to appear
the Greek Noumenia

light breaking along the edge
the Hebrew Rosh Chodesh

waxing crescent moon
the Arabic Alhilal

first quarter moon
the Hawaiian Ole Kulua

half-moon in Kenyan villages
the Swahili Nusu-mwezi

harvest full moon in North America
the Algonquin kagakone kizis

full moon beginning to wane
the Australian islander's eip meb

waning crescent moon
the Japanese Kagentsu

dark of the moon over India

the Hindu Amavasya

Charles Maxim Bernstein, Miami, Miami-Dade County, Florida

Phases of the Moon

Is it the phases of the moon

that harnesses carnal ache

we writhe around entwinned

until our bodies quake

Illuminating through

the floor to ceiling pane

our nakedness glistens

underneath the wax and wane

Inhibition falters

with its fullness at height

body to body heaving

'til the morning light

In its shadow

we lie in darkness, me and you

abed a sea of tranquility

our love is anew

Cynthia Uzzolino, Miramar, Broward County, Florida

Poetry in Porcelain

Yes, every once in a while, even writers catch a lucky break.

Yes, we do have our serendipitous moments.

And to my surprise, one week ago serendipity hit me in the
aisle of a Cracker Barrel.

You see, I'm the SFWA chairman of our joint 35th
Anniversary, Howard Camner Poems
Landing on the Moon Christmas party.

What an endeavor!

And one of my assignments is to look for stuff related to our
theme, "The Moon."

So I'm walking down that Cracker Barrel aisle and I find a
display of moon-related stuff.

"Wow. How fortuitous," I think and I wonder, "Was this
display here because of the eclipse? Who knows?"

But as I examine the tchotchkes and a smile eclipses my face.
My eyes spy upon a box of
porcelain salt & pepper shakers.

Not your ordinary run of the mill shakers but ones shaped like
the Earth, the Moon, a rocket,
and an alien.

A blue and green earth which highlights the continents, a pink
moon pockmarked with craters, a
black and white rocket with one porthole and four fins and a
scary red moon alien.

Before my eyes, Howard Camner's miraculous story has been
told in porcelain.

On Earth, Howard crafts his poems.

Then a rocket flies them to the Moon.

Where aliens read them and think that our SFWA member is
one hell-of-a-poet.

I buy half of the box of these salt & pepper shakers:

As gifts for Howard and his wife;
As party favors for the folks that plan and run the event;

As door prizes;

As a prop for this story.

So my fellow writers and poets, remember no matter where
you are, be on the lookout for
serendipity.

For she may inspire you to write a poem or a story that ends
up on the surface of the Moon.

Mort Laitner, Cooper City, Broward County, Florida

Same Moon

Hi Randy.

You and I have the same moon.

You are in Tokyo, I am in Fort Lauderdale but we have the same moon.

We see it at the same time, but you are waking up and I am putting on my nightshirt.

For you it is tomorrow, always one day ahead

You are always 14 hours ahead of me

On New Years, we are even in different years for part of the day.

I hope you come back here someday because I miss you.

I have made a good life for myself.

I am happy

But to be honest there is a big hole

I have gotten used to holidays, restaurants and dinner parties alone

I like to live alone

I don't want to do the Jewish guilt thing with you about how I miss you

But I do

For now, we talk, we text, we send pictures

You come here to visit

We like shopping at Nordstrom Rack

We like Greek food

We like to load up at Costco

My next car is going to be a Nissan

I have had 3 of them and my warranty runs out next year on

the Mercedes Benz

No way am I paying out of pocket for repairs on that

Now that you work for Nissan and I am going to get another

one

We will have that in common

And we will have the same moon

Love from Mother

August 10, 2024

Anita Mitchell, Fort Lauderdale, Broward County, Florida

Strawberry Super Moon

Even moongazers hope to see a comet,
at the least a shooting star, exploded light
dead for eons, reaching us now.

Is it hope that causes us to look up,
sit outside with the mosquitoes
watching, for just the barest quiver?

This isn't about the moon, or any moon,
It's more like longing. How it settles on your skin
like moonlight, like burnt sugar.

I suppose "mooning" is a sort of longing,
so maybe this is about the moon, after all.
Or a new world we could escape to—

How we navigate this earth is an enigma
How we claim to cherish but act to destroy.
I am having issues with my heart, how it breaks

Too easily these days, watching events unfold
like origami sculptures, made of nothing
more solid than this paper, which crumples
easily, then burns to ash.

How we claim to cherish but act to destroy.
I am having issues with my heart, how it breaks

Too easily these days, watching events unfold
like origami sculptures, made of nothing
more solid than this paper, which crumples
easily, then burns to ash.

Barbra Nightingale, Miami, Miami-Dade County, Florida

Amy

Richard Frost, West Hollywood, Los Angeles County, California

The Lunar Library

Fly Me to the Moon, where stardust quills write – in the ink of constellations, our stories ignite.

Prologue:

In the not-so-distant future, aboard the *Artemis II Voyager*, a spaceship destined for the Moon, the peculiar cargo was nestled in the cargo bay – a shiny silver disk etched with humanity's collective wisdom to preserve among the stars. It was only the size of a U.S. silver dollar but carried a huge message. Captain Ellie "Quill" Melasi, a former librarian turned astronaut, guarded her precious delivery on board.

Chapter 1: The Cosmic Archive

The miniature disk held more than mere data. It cradled an anthology of stories, poems, and essays – a Lunar Library. Quill imagined its message spinning through space, carrying the echoes of ancient scribes, forgotten civilizations, and modern dreamers alike.

"Why the moon?" her copilot, Ethan, asked. "Why not Mars or beyond?"

"Because," Quill replied, "the Moon is our closest neighbor, yet it holds the farthest reaches of the imagination. I think it was brilliant that NASA decided to plant our literary flag there."

Chapter 2: The Power of Words

As the *Artemis II Voyager* glided down toward the lunar surface, Quill reflected on the value of literacy. She'd seen firsthand how a child's eyes widened as they opened their first book. And how a grandmother's laughter echoed through her memoir's pages.

"Literacy," Quill mused, "is the warp speed of the mind. It propels us beyond our limitations and connects us across epochs.

Chapter 3: The Lunar Legacy

On the Moon, Quill and Ethan stepped out, the underside of their boots crunching as they walked on a billion years worth of tiny silver-grey moonstones, imprinting lunar haikus on their minds as they went: Silver-grey on the crescent glows – craters hold lunar haikus, echoes of poets.

They placed the shiny disk near the *Tranquility Base* – a nod to Astronauts Armstrong and Aldrin. Quill thought, *the Moon keeps its secrets – ancient footprints, Apollo whispers, and lunar geology.*

She could still remember Armstrong's words as he stepped on the Moon. *"That's one small step for man, one giant leap for mankind."* She was glad she'd put that quote on the disk for future generations to ponder.

Quill pointed to the shiny disk and whispered, "This is our legacy."

"Why?" Ethan asked. "Why preserve these words?"

"Because," Quill said, "they're our cosmic breadcrumbs. They help guide us home and remind us of who we are."

Chapter 4: The Celestial Readers

Back on the ship, Quill activated the disk's holographic interface to activate the disk on the Moon. It came to life. Words danced – Shakespearean sonnets, Martian chronicles, quantum physics treatises, Keats, Dickinson, and Robert Frost's *The Road Not Taken*. Quill chuckled, thinking of his words… "and I, I took the road less traveled by, and that has made all the difference." How apropos for this mission.

Ethan broke into her thoughts when he suddenly grinned, threw his arms wide, and shouted. "We're like the lunar librarians of the cosmos!"

"Indeed," Quill agreed. "And someday, a lunar explorer will stumble upon humanity's disk. They'll read our stories, our hopes, and our follies."

Chapter 5. The Infinite Possibilities

As the *Artemis II Voyager* prepared to leave for Earth, Quill whispered to the Moon, "May our words inspire future generations. May they spark curiosity, empathy, and wonder." And so the shiny disk spun in its protective case on the Moon – its cosmic compass pointing towards infinity. Quill knew that literacy wasn't just about decoding squiggles but of the universe itself – a syllabic symphony of human existence... a testament to the power of words.

Beverly Melasi-Haag, Miami, Miami-Dade County, Florida

The Lunar Beasts

Deep in a crater blasted many megaannum prior, during our solar system's infancy, jumped a rabbit. This snow-white critter lept, past the high crater rim, before falling gently and repeating. Between his long ears waited a toad, who sprung when the rabbit reached apex, to see ever farther.

With their leaps, both watched the colored Earth, vibrant sister of the moon. A wolf approached the two, yawning, then asked, "Find them yet?"

"No." said the toad.

The rabbit added, "But the humans will arrive soon!"

The three reached the rim, standing united, watching the world away. The wolf said, "They will regret coming."

"Absurd!" said the rabbit.

"Perhaps not." commented a doe, kicking up dust as she neared. "I miss our first home."

"Wish to return?" prompted the toad.

"Never. We fulfill our duty here. But I long for my saunters around the Peloponnese, outwitting and outrunning hunters and hounds alike."

"The rivers of Yunnan." reminisced the toad. "The bank-mud ripe with insects."

"But our palaces!" said the rabbit. "Our domains built in craters, statues of basalt, porticoes of dust! Our homes here will enchant the humans."

"For a time." said the wolf. "Their excitement, their glee, will fog their memories. But once accustomed, they will romanticize Earth, forget its fires and flaws, then long to return."

The four sat, observing the world against a panorama of void and stars. The toad asked, "Where is he?"

"Here." answered the bull, a vigorous beast of crescent horns. "Finished plowing my fields, then reorganizing my palace, to prepare for visitors."

The toad asked, "Will the humans, if they colonize here, demand your strength for construction?"

The bull snorted, then said, "They better not. My terrestrial kin and I did more than enough for humanity. Their precious, shiny machines will lug their loads from now on."

The wolf said, "Another reason to avoid the newcomers."

The rabbit said, "You are never full. Give you a feast, you demand why not two."

"One of us must remain wary."

The rabbit agreed there. The five witnessed calamity after disaster befall their earthbound relatives. Floods, fires, freezes, flames, and beyond. Their position afforded peace, quiet at last, but detached observance of life. Their terrestrial bloodkin went hunted, pursued, hungry, persecuted, and a thousand woes. Ever competing against a species both master and lord of Earth.

The rabbit asked, "Remember the Endangered Species Act, and the Bern Convention?"

The other four did. Back then, they celebrated the victories across their five palaces.

The toad said, "The banning of river dumping."

The bull said, "Mechanized farming."

The doe said, "National preserves."

The rabbit waved a white paw at the wolf. The canine said, "My kind's hunting still occurs in Russia. And my Japanese cousins perished a mere century ago."

"To be fair, you are frightful. Requires time to know your heart, adapt to your cold, just as the newcomers must accustom to our moon."

The five observed their worlds. The doe said, "The humans call canines their greatest friends."

The wolf said, "Dogs are mangy descendants of mine, embarrassing."

The bull said, "Well, that mangy family first achieved planetary orbit." The keepers silenced, remembering Laika. Then the bull continued, "Humans will certainly bring dogs. Your boredom will vanish."

The wolf's ears rose. She did lack playmates on the moon. For her claws and sharp teeth, the others refused to play.

From then on, the five waited, amused and accompanied by each other, until the lander touched down. So the moon beasts heralded the coming age, the future.

Giancarlo Diago Cevallos, Palmetto Bay, Miami-Dade, Florida

The Man In The Moon, For Real

He lived on my street under an alias
I met him one time, by accident
When he introduced himself, he said, "If a man has to tell you
his name, he ain't nobody"
Then he told me his name and handed me his card

When the moon was full, I would see him sitting on his roof
with a photo negative of an 8 x 10 headshot and a flashlight
projecting his face on the moon's surface

He was the Man in the Moon for real
I know it
He told me so one time, by accident

When he introduced himself, he said that people who have
nothing to say,
say it the loudest
(He said that very loudly)

He rarely left his house except to buy cheese, toilet paper, and
batteries for his flashlight

He always regretted having a life full of regrets
so he lived on my street under an alias
Didn't want anyone to know who he was

except when he introduced himself

He was the Man in the Moon for real
I know it

It's been 28 years since he fell off his roof and died by accident
and I still see his face on the moon's surface, even today (at
night)

Go figure

Howard Camner, Miami, Miami-Dade County, Florida

The Moon

Apollo 11 reshapes thousands of thoughts and beliefs
on the earth,
sprawling on the lunar lap.

I wish I could collect those pre-Apollo eyes
from the sand
and show them the moon is not God.
But they belong to
the same species living in peace of ignorance today.

Fanaticism is a fireball.
True belief illuminates like the moon.
Prayer prevents immoral anarchy.

Not a reflection of sunlight,
it's nature's solace spreading over the wounds.

How differently it shines in science and literature!
It's as veracious as a breccia
that the moon is dusty, gritty, and abrasive.
But that hare is more beautiful than the rocky truth.

Fabiyas M V, Thrissur District, Kerala State, India

The Moon And I Walk The Dog

The moon and I walk the dog this evening
Little Fiona happy to be out, even on a leash
With just enough moonlight to show her things
On the ground, in the grass off the sidewalk
Abandoned wrappers, broken twigs
Turds from those who have passed before

She is a chihuahua sized dog but not so obnoxious
With the coloring of a Doberman
And a conception I dread to think about
Any combination of male and female shocking
While I look around for other dog-walkers
And Cyclists, they are the worst
Coming quickly up behind me in silence
Like I don't belong there
That's why the moon comforts me
Letting me see, letting me sense
The presence of others

The moon, the moon, gloriously indifferent
Like God, high in the sky
And completely indifferent to my walking
I talk to God often now in my later years
And pray constantly that He does not answer

Just refer me to the moon above, full or new
Offering me freedom, walking my little dog

Neil Crabtree, Palmetto Bay, Miami-Dade County, Florida

The Moon Changing Me

Spherical orb of the night
With your alabaster glow,
You pull me in
with amazement.

You make the tides sing
in the highest key
And every four weeks,
you show up in full,
illuminating the night
and all its nocturnal delights.
You are a child of Nature.

As I watch you,
something moves inside me.
Heart beating faster now
as scarlet blood pumps heavily
through tired, aging veins.
A new life unfolds within me.

I close my eyes.
I realize that
my transformation
will never be complete
without you.

And you, with eternal power,

transform my soul.

I drop to my knees

and bow down in honor

of your majestic awe.

So, keep doing your great work,

you mesmerizing beauty.

You have changed me

in ways that I need to be...

And as long as I can see,

I will always gaze at you

and appreciate

your worth.

Billy Jones, Miami, Miami-Dade County, Florida

The Moon: Fear, Science, and Love

When I was a little girl, I used to look up at the sky and wonder, "What is that big, scary rock doing up there?" I was afraid of the huge ball hanging from the ceiling of my limited universe.

Didn't anyone worry that it might come crashing down on us one day? I thought.

The stars, on the other hand, didn't scare me. I saw them as cute sparkles of light on the ceiling of my world.

I now feel that my fear of the moon was rooted in my inability to understand how the moon could religiously show up every night, always in different shapes. The one that scared me the most was the full moon. Full moon, werewolves! Oh no! Could it have been because of the role of the moon in mystery movies? Then, I read this spooky quote in one of my dad's books.

"The night walked down the sky with the moon in her hand." Frederic Lawrence Knowles

I never shared this fear with my parents. I'm sure they would have shed some light on my worries.

One day in school during my science class, the teacher mentioned, "The moon is responsible for the tides." And I thought, *So what? What is the big deal about tides? Are we risking being crushed by that huge ball so that the oceans go up and down?*

The science teacher went on and on about tides. *Tides? Of all the things in the world are you hung up on the stupid tides?* I thought.

"Tides are important to humans for several reasons, including their impact on navigation, fishing, coastal management, and energy production." She kept talking and driving me dizzy, "Number 1. For Navigation: Tides influence the depth of water in harbors, estuaries, and along coastlines," blah, blah, blah she continued. "Number 2. For Fishing and Aquaculture: Tides affect the distribution and behavior of marine life. Number 3. For Coastal Management: Understanding tides is essential for managing coastal areas, preventing erosion," blah… blah…blah… "Number 4. For Energy Production…" My head was exploding! *Am I supposed to write all this down?* I kept scribbling in my notebook, but nothing made any sense to me. "Number 5. For Flood Prediction and Management… And number 6. For Recreation, blah, blah, blah."

My hand was cramping on me from so much writing. *I do not care about this! And… do I have to know all this for the test? Oh no!!*

At this point, I told my parents, "I hate the moon. We are risking that big rock to crush us one day, and we don't do anything about it?" To which my parents responded, "The moon is important to life on Earth, and besides…, your mom and I fell in love under the light of a full romantic moon."

"Under the moon? Ugh…" I responded. "How were you able to know where to stand? And weren't you afraid that it could come crashing on your head?" So, my father continued. "Also, let me remind you of Budha's words:"

Three things cannot be long hidden: the sun, the moon, and the truth." Buddha

My teenage sister who overheard our conversation said, "I agree with you, sister. The moon is spooky especially the full moon." She emphasized with a grin on her face. "And do you know why? Well…" she continued, "some boys even turn into werewolves under the full moon!"

"Oh no! Is this true, Dad?" I replied in panic. But she continued… "Have you heard George Carlin's quote?"

"There are nights when the wolves are silent and only the moon howls." George Carlin

"When is the next full moon? I'm hiding under my bed and stay there forever!" I replied screaming while my sister laughed and my father scolded her for scaring me to death.

A year later, in my science class, the teacher said, "Who knows how the moon was formed?" *Oh no! Here we go again with the stupid moon,* I thought. However, I did not want to get in trouble, so I stayed quiet. Then, she continued, "The Moon formed about 4.5 billion years ago after a Mars-sized body collided with Earth, resulting in debris that eventually coalesced to form the Moon."

Debri! No wonder I hate the moon, it's just a ball of garbage. And then she continued, "The Moon helps to stabilize the Earth's axial tilt. This stability is crucial for maintaining a relatively stable climate over geological time scales." *Now I'm confused*, I thought. She continued, "Who can list the phases of the moon and explain why these phases exist?" Of course, there is always the nerdy student in class who knows it all. So, she responded.

Later that year, in my Social Studies class I heard the teacher saying, "The Moon has been crucial for navigation and timekeeping, while the phases of the Moon helped early civilizations create calendars and navigate the seas. Additionally, the Moon has been a source of inspiration in literature, mythology, and art across various cultures." *Oh wow! I can't believe so much stupidity.* I thought.

At the age of fifteen, my life took a dramatic change of course. During a class dance party, the cutest boy in the school asked me to dance. Of course, as you can imagine I was in heaven! After several rounds of rock and roll and other lively pieces of music, we stepped outside onto a small balcony in search of fresh air. Then, he said, "Have you seen how beautiful the moon is tonight!" I thought, *Oh no!* Not the moon again! But…, I stopped to reflect. *Could this be what my parents were referring to?* However, to my surprise, I replied, "I agree, the moon is beautiful tonight!" *What am I saying?* I thought, *I have always hated the moon!*

Years passed when I realized that maybe my fear of the moon was rooted in my ignorance of the laws of the universe and the forces that keep celestial objects in orbit. A sudden surge of interest ignited within me, sparking a deep passion for science, particularly in Physics and scientific exploration, when I learned that not only the Moon's surface contains helium-3! A potential fuel for the so much needed future nuclear fusion reactors and that the presence of water ice in permanently shadowed craters at the lunar poles could be vital for future human exploration and habitation; I was hooked!

Wow! I thought. *Maybe I'm starting to like the moon! And I'm starting to love science!* Knowledge is like the moonlight that brightens the darkness of ignorance.

However, I have to confess that up to this day, my favorite part of the moon remains stepping onto the balcony with my boyfriend and feeling the love under its soft, glowing light.

"So, we'll go no more a roving So late into the night, Though the heart be still as loving, And the moon be still as bright." Lord Byron

Gladys A Barrio, Miami, Miami-Dade County, Florida

The Moon Obscured

I thought I saw it
like that stickman that keeps reappearing
from way back when
it was green cheese
and the old troll in a shack

Now it's cloaked in clouds
and raising werewolves
where swamps freeze, moss pink blooms,
and the white hare hides
where bones cross and Soma spills

I thought I saw it
like Rona with her bucket of rain
and the old mother rocking out west
where lunacy prevails and antlers form
where a family is fed on a single grain of rice
where magic is not magic
at all

I thought I saw it

clear as day just after midnight

but there's an eye missing and half a grin

there's something more but I don't know what

like secrets in plain view

that still remain secrets

Howard Camner, Miami, Miami-Dade County, Florida

Phases

Charles Maxim Bernstein, Miami, Miami-Dade County, Florida

The Neglected Moon
after Baudelaire

Moon, our mothers and fathers gaped
at you, their eyes full of you parading
up the blue-black sky, stars and planets draped
behind. And now, illuminating

our triumphant back rooms, we sleep (small planets
ourselves), tired from love, slack-jawed, our teeth
gleaming and white like you. O shine on your poets
stymied at their papers, and snakes that writhe

in open fields, full of desire. But to shine
on that handsome boy who refuses to age
and sleeps till noon….well…and you, tracing lines

round your eyes before the mirror, yellow frock
disheveled, rubbing just a little rouge
on nipples he wouldn't fondle or suck….

Steve Kronen, Miami, Miami-Dade County, Florida

To The Moon in Joy

Until the day she died, my mother kept an 8 x 10 framed photo on her desk of when she saw the Apollo 11 rocket launch on its way to the moon.

It was July 16, 1969.

At the press site, she met famous newsmen of the time. She even saw Walter Cronkite who covered the NASA event for the CBS Evening News.

He reported all the breaking news including John F. Kennedy's death in 1963. NASA renamed its rocket launch site Cape Kennedy after the President's assassination. And it remained that name for ten years to honor the man who opened the race to the moon.

Also, at the press site were the photographers and reporters from much bigger newspapers and broadcast outlets from around the world.

There was the team from The New York Times, The Houston Chronicle, The San Francisco Chronicle, and even Astronaut Neil Armstrong's Ohio home newspaper The Wapakoneta Daily News.

There were reporters and photographers speaking languages my mother had never heard. The world came together in hope and delight.

My mother, Bea Moss, a revered journalist and editor, represented The Miami Herald's tiny community outreach newspaper The Coral Gables Times and The Guide. She later wrote a personal column about her adventure.

My little brother and I were nearby, camped out with family friends, at a safe spot a few miles away. I remember it was hot and I wore shorts.

We all saw the Saturn V rocket lift off. My mother, who was much closer, told us later that she wanted to push it up and off Launch Pad 39.

It was so slow, she said whenever she remembered the flames, the tower pulling away, the giant beast roaring into the beyond.

The framed black and white photo shows her smiling a smile I rarely saw.

She was there. With all the men. As a woman who early on broke glass ceilings, through tears that flowed almost nightly about the career barricades put up before her.

As a news reporter, of course, she brought a part time photographer, Parks Masterson. Bea called him Bat, I think because he went to bat for her. Who knows?

My mother died in 2010, and I can no longer call her to ask a question about family history, life, advice, help, Star Trek.

Bat told me their editor gave them press passes to the launch. He said he really enjoyed working with my mom. In

2019, he returned to the renamed Cape Canaveral for the 50th anniversary of the first moon launch.

I know my mother would have been there too.

But I can look at that photo of her, with the giant Vehicle Assembly Building in the background, and feel her joy.

She saw history. In her heart she was still the little girl from Chicago whose lawyer father died suddenly. Whose mother then dragged her away to Florida where she worked placing classified ads for The St. Petersburg Times.

Until she got a break in a move to Miami. Weekly, she walked in freelance stories for The Coral Gables Times and The Guide. She was finally hired.

And the rest is her history, and mine.

When I look up at the moon on clear nights, I think of the flags there, the footprints, the craters, the Sea of Tranquility where Apollo 11 landed, and the hopes and dreams and determination of many.

But it always reminds me of my Mom.

Christina Moss Mayo, Coral Gables, Miami-Dade County, Florida

Tokyo Games 2020

Shining star, Katie Moon
pole vaulted herself
to the moon
as she reached
for Olympic gold.

Connie Goodman-Milone, Miami, Miami-Dade County, Florida

Trashing the Moon and Mars

Flags fade on the face of the moon,
footprints are lost in its dust,
landers and rovers litter the landscape,
bags of Astronaut poop could bust.

Two golf balls landed somewhere
on that pristine lunar course,
with lower gravity levels
they flew without much force.

A falcon feather and hammer,
proved Galileo's theory correct.
Photo of an astronaut's family
was left with a note on the back.

Mars is the first of the planets
to accumulate earthborn scrap.
We figured out how to get there,
not how to bring the junk back.

Orbiters, rovers, and helicopter
will circle, probe and hover
until the mechanical lifespans
signal their searching is over.
Every small step for man,

each giant leap for mankind,

left trash where no one had gone before

for future space travelers to find

And let's not forget our home planet,

the tons still orbiting Earth,

what went up, will eventually come down,

threatening satellite networks

"Take only memories, leave only footprints,"

Chief Seattle said long ago.

But we trashed the Moon and Mars,

we'll keep trashing wherever we go.

Pat Bonner Milone, Redland, Miami-Dade County, Florida

Waning Crescent

Sky has eaten Moon
down to the rind
Dawn's yellow glow
obscures its lunar shine

As the gossamer sliver
fades slowly from sight,
clouds fringe with gold
in Sun's morning light

Tides with their rhythms,
seas ebbing and flooding,
prove Moon is still out there,
still pushing and pulling

Pat Bonner Milone, Redland, Miami-Dade County, Florida

What Does the Moon Mean to Me?

Unlike many people who believe the moon to be a source of love and romance, I believe the moon to be a representation of science and exploration. Once of my earliest memories is of my family gathered around a TV console watching the lunar landing and the astronauts safe return home. As a child, I remember science classes where we studied how the moon controlled the tides, and to an extent, the climate on Earth. Who could forget the excitement of the school field trips to the Museum of Science and the Planetarium where we were transported among the moon and stars.

Another source of joy during my scholastic years were the eclipses both lunar and solar. In high-school physics, I studied its gravitational pulls. As I grew up, my fascination with science and mathematics continued, which solidified my choice to study engineering. During my college years, I worked for NOAA flying on hurricane reconnaissance aircraft. After I graduated with my degree in electrical engineering, I was somewhat lost as to where I wanted to work. Many companies in the South Florida area were not hiring. After much reflection and recollection, I looked up at the moon. The answer became crystal clear – the space program. I applied to NASA and its government contractors. I was fortunate to have received multiple offers, from which I chose NASA to begin my engineering career. There, I worked on the communications systems for Shuttle and payload processing at Kennedy Space Center, and I would drive by the Saturn V rocket on display by the Launch Control Center when I worked the Shuttle launches. The site of the Saturn V rocket, which was used to launch astronauts to the moon, always brought a smile to my face as I remembered the little girl who was obsessed with science and the moon.

Monica DeZulueta, Miami, Miami-Dade County, Florida

Winter Moon

On a sleepless night,
my cat squats on my shoulder
gnawing on my dreams.

Awake or dreaming,
I leave my son's empty room,
his bed still unmade.

Under the moon's spell,
I watch my father's shadow
circling the lake's rim.

He walks with purpose
like the man I once adored--
and not ten years dead.

Brimming with questions,
I whisper, "Dada, please tell
me, will my son live?"

While toads bellow, he
laughs. "That I'm dead doesn't mean
I know everything."

"We are all living,"
he says, "We're just thin membranes
to eternity"

Around the lake's edge
the sound of toads and crickets
undone by moonlight

At the hospital
doctors greet me by the stairs.
I'm a veteran.

Through rain-streaked windows
on a cramped hospital chair—
no stars in the sky

Nurses come and go
on nights when the only thing
longer is my grief.

The world is a blur.
After waiting for sunrise
my breath grows shorter.

My son's fever breaks.

I lift my head from prayers.

The first sign of light.

Geoffrey Philp, North Miami Beach, Miami-Dade County, Florida

Wishes Under the Full Moon

"When I'm old and grey-

I pray my mind is invaded by beautiful memories.

Of a life well lived and that continues to be.

I look up to the sky and get a glimpse of the man sitting atop

of the Bella Luna - does he look down at me?

For stress dissipates when passion within is set free-

So many who have gone before, and broken the barriers so we

could see.

A life of no regrets and where my mind's eye can be free-

My purpose unfold as it continues to call to me -

Go where you are loved to serve founded in generosity.

All the faces I've known, the souls that gave me much glee-

And when I seek peace - I'll sit under the moon by the

beautiful sea.

Facing the ocean-

Under the orb's bright light, I write wishes in the sand with

words of clarity.

I'll worship at the hand of gratitude for the kindness presented

to me.

My blessings foretold when I came as a small baby -

My spirit courageously sings aloud a beautiful legacy.

A lunar ritual as I take my place beside the waves and clouds

for what feels like eternity.

Under the full moon, pondering what wonder through space &
its discoveries,
There I know we are truly blessed and excited to see,
Looking out as the waves carry my wishes like the space
explorers traveling to a sea of tranquility.
Anything is possible through innovation & creativity!"

Meg Nocero, Miami, Miami-Dade County, Florida

Dolly Attacks

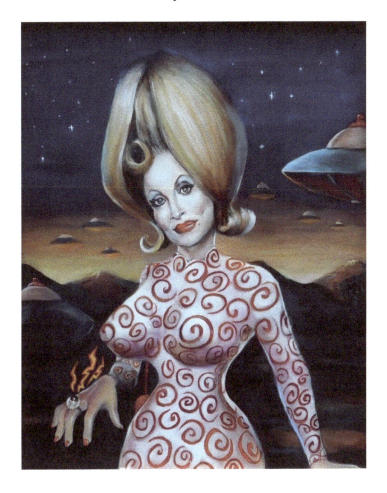

Richard Frost, West Hollywood, Los Angeles County, California

Lunar Codex Party Planning is Hard

I read the latest Lunar Codex posting concerning the Polaris launch. It said, "The Polaris launch is scheduled with Griffin for November 2024, with a possible delay to February 2025. Schedule changes in the space industry are not uncommon – space is hard."

Well, you know what else is hard?
Party planning.

Party planning without knowing when Polaris is going to launch or the lander is going to touch the surface, that's tough. How are we going to book a venue? How are we going to draw in a crowd?

Well, anyway the South Florida Writers Association created this game plan.

I know what you're thinking, "What's he bellyaching about? In the words of Tonto, "Kemosabe, party many moons away." Ya Tonto, it's only May and we've got until February to pull this party off.

But SFWA members are moonstruck, obsessive-compulsive Earthlings. Like the Boy Scouts, our motto is "Be Prepared."

So here's our agenda: We sing "Fly Me To The Moon," or "Got A One-Way Ticket to the Moon," or "Blue Moon."

Members read poems or short stories or recite their favorite Moon quotes. Here's mine, "Don't tell me the sky's the limit when there are footprints on the Moon." —Paul Brandt.

Salt and Pepper Shakers, shaped like the Moon, the Earth, a rocket ship and an alien are awarded as prizes for best costumes, or best moon-themed poetry or best lunar short story or best quote about the Moon.

Menu includes crescent rolls, moon pies, and moon cheese.

A Moon-shaped cake with craters and a plastic satellite and an alien resting on its surface and the words, "Congrats Howard and the Lunar Codex" written in black on the white frosting.

Paper cups filled with Moon juice (ingredients remain a top secret) are raised for a hearty toast to Howard and the Lunar Codex.

If our venue sells alcohol beverages, our assortment of drinks ranges from moonshine to Blue Moon beer to blue moon martinis to amber moon and to angry moon. Who knew that so many drinks have moon in their names?

So you can see, we have one-hell-of-a-party planned. But don't forget, schedule changes in the party-planning business are not uncommon—therefore, party planning is hard.

Mort Laitner, Cooper City, Broward County, Florida

EPILOGUE

"Don't tell me the sky's the limit when there are footprints on the moon." Paul Brandt

When Howard Camner asked me to join him in co-editing "The Sea of Tranquility---A Literary Journal" I was blown away. My writings on a disc, in a time capsule, stationed on the surface of the Moon, housed in the Lunar Codex along with the works of some 35,000 contemporary artists from 253 countries. territories, and indigenous nations.

My footprint on the moon. The word "wow" really doesn't cut it.

What an honor. And we all know that with honor comes responsibility.

Lucky for me I had been editor-in-chief of the six-volume set of public health anthologies entitled "Healthy Stories."

While I worked at the Miami-Dade Department of Public Health, I learned the meaning of team building, deadlines, teamwork, and selecting quality over quantity.

I developed an assignment matrix, a project chart, a submission binder, and a daily activity log.

And we met our goals and accomplished our mission.

As the poems and short stories appeared on my desktop, I loved reading how each poet or short story writer related to the moon.

On behalf of Howard and myself, I want to thank our assistant editors and compilers, Monica DeZulueta, Neil Crabtree, and Travis Laitner, for their brilliant work and assistance.

Finally, I want to thank Dr. Samuel Peralta, the creator of Lunar Codex dreams. Where 35,000 small artistic steps have lead to one giant leap for contemporary art. You have given members of the South Florida Writers Association and the "Old Guard" a place in history and a thrill of a lifetime. On behalf of all of us thanks for putting our footprints on the moon.

Mission Accomplished.

Mort Laitner-Cooper City, Florida-August 27, 2024

ABOUT THE AUTHORS

Carla Albano is a 30-year resident of South Florida. Carla, an attorney, was also a local business owner for 25 years. Upon retiring in 2017, she began writing. Her first book, **Soul of a Swimmer** was published in 2021. The book is currently being adapted into a play, slated to premiere in early 2025. Carla enjoys writing both fiction and non-fiction and mentoring fellow writers.

Jo Avent grew up in the UK and (after stints in Spain, France, and Australia) she 'met a boy' and ended up in the US. After nearly 20 years in Chicago, she is delighted to call Miami home, where she lives with her husband, their two children and their retired dog. She is rediscovering creative writing after a career spanning corporate America and the tech start up world.

Swati Bagga, born in India, is a proud mother of loving, caring sons Yayati and Pulastya, dear pets Buntoo, Ahri, Sheroo, Bhaloo. Forever, deeply loving her dearest soulmate Davinder "ji". Proud daughter, sister, aunt of Puri, Giri, Bagga, Sharma, Das, Goyal, Rathore families and friends. Blessed Miami Southridge teacher for students, colleagues "Lunch Bunch 4Eva". A God loving earthling.

Dr. Gladys A. Barrio, born in Cuba and raised in Puerto Rico, now resides in Miami, FL. She holds a Ph.D. in Chemistry from the University of Miami and has authored over twenty-five scientific publications. Dr. Barrio served as Executive Director and Science Supervisor for Miami-Dade County Public Schools and taught Chemistry and Methods of Teaching Science at various universities.

Charles Maxim Bernstein (born 1950 in Miami, Florida) is a contemporary artist who writes poems to accompany his visual images. His paintings span a wide range of styles, subjects, and media. He began to explore digital art in 1981 and he has continued to explore its creative possibilities.

His work can be found in the permanent collections of Miami Dade College and the University of Miami Lowe Art Museum.

Mark Bonaparte, gifted with curiosity and a thirst for learning, spends his life creating beautiful works in many crafts including watercolor, welding, writing, photography, programming and poetry. Mark views everything as an act of his expansion, exploration and self expression. He advocates for compassionate action and recognition of the innate preciousness in every one and everything.

Dr. Linda M. Campbell is an educator with experience as a principal and teacher in secondary education. She is also a business leader and adjunct doctoral chair/advisor at a major American university. Linda Campbell is the author of "Blocks of Time", a book on time to task management. The book is a self-portrait of Dr. Campbell's use of time blocks both professionally and personally.

Howard Camner is a Pulitzer Prize-nominated poet and author of 25 books. A founder of New York's Literary Outlaws, Camner was nominated for Poet Laureate of Florida (1980) and named "Best Poet in Miami" (New Times "Best of Miami" edition 2007). He received the Marquis Lifetime Achievement Award for Literary Arts and was inducted into the MDC Hall of Fame. Camner's major works are housed in the Emerson Archives.

Giancarlo Diago Cevallos is a proud amateur: author, pianist, historian, dog walker. He loves animals, the ocean, and sweets. In his free time, enjoys a good book. Even writes them too. Passionate explorer, collector of art, professional sneezer. Vice-President of the South Florida Writers Association

Neil Crabtree serves on the Board of Directors of the South Florida Writers Association. He provided compiling help and editorial advice during the development of Sea of Tranquility. His books include: Believable Lies, Smuggler's Return, The Barricades of Heaven and the upcoming Not Dead Yet. His blog is: miamiwritersandbooks.blogspot.com; web: floridaneil.com.

Raining Deer aka Jeanette Stephens-El has written for several newspapers and was creator of "Southern Dawn Magazine". She was a founder the Pan African Bookfest & Cultural Conference. She has served as executive director of the African American Caribbean Cultural Arts Commission and on boards of various arts organizations.

Lenny DellaRocca is founding publisher and editor of South Florida Poetry Journal-SoFloPoJo. His poetry has appeared in Denver Quarterly, Cimirron Review, I-70 Review, One, Nimrod and others. He is an editor of Chameleon Chimera, An Anthology of Florida Poets (Purple Ink press). He has five poetry collections on Earth.

Monica DeZulueta, Ph.D., is an author of techno-thrillers which feature women engineers and scientists. After a long career as an engineer working at NASA, NOAA, Microsoft and Coulter, she pursued her dream of becoming a novelist. Monica found writing to be a creative outlet to her engineering and academic work. Monica is profiled in two books, *Latinnovating* and *Steam Powered Girls.*

Rita Fidler Dorn (Ricki) is a retired college writing professor, former news reporter, and published author of four poetry books, one collection of essays, and an eclectic tome. She is passionate about poetry, is a word game addict and a grammar guru as well as a dedicated member of South Florida Writers Association. Born on July 8, Ricki is a moon child.

Regine Rayevsky Fisher of Miami was born in Moscow, where she received the equivalent of a Bachelor of Arts degree. Upon emigrating to the United States, she entered Columbia University and received an M.F.A. in 1993. Regine has taught piano, voice, Russian literature, and has been drawing and painting throughout those years. She has been illustrating her own stories.

Fabiyas M V is an acute observer of the world, a passionate lover of humanity, and a harsh critic of human follies. His poems thrill us with self-reflective insights, sooth us with compassionate emotions and make us shiver with his thoughtful warnings. He uses stark, uncanny and unsettling imagery to portray the decadence of our time. But his poems are also a testimony to the fact that he transcends the mundane world to forge a cosmic vision.

Richard Frost is a renowned artist who refers to his artistic style as "tweaked realism". An art critic proclaimed Frost's work as "Norman Rockwell meets the Twilight Zone". He is widely recognized as one of the most innovative artists working today. A graduate of the Otis Parsons Art Institute, Frost lives and paints in Los Angeles.

Connie Goodman-Milone, MSW is a writer and hospice volunteer. She is a past president and serves as Community

Relations Director of SFWA. She contributes letters to the editor to the Miami Herald. Her poetry has appeared in numerous journals and anthologies. Connie was given a VITAS BEST Award in 2021. She received a Marquis Who's Who Humanitarian Award in 2017 and 2023-24.

Mary Greenwood has been an Attorney, Arbitrator, Law Professor, Ebay Mediator and Personnel Manager. She has written: How to Negotiate Like a Pro, How to Mediate Like a Pro, and How to Interview Like a Pro. She remembers the first Moon Landing; Blue Moon is one of her favorite songs; and she loves a Full Moon.

Susana Jiménez-Mueller is a Cuban American writer, storyteller, and podcaster. She is the producer and host of *Cuban Stories on The Green Plantain*, a Cuban story project podcast, and the author of several books. She writes prose and poetry about love, family, and the quotidian. Her avocation is producing audio recordings for Life Story writers at the Bloomingdale Regional Library in Valrico, Florida.

Billy P. Jones, Ph.D., is the author of the Everyday Folks book series, a collection of fictional stories based in South Florida. He is also the creator and host of Everyday Folks Radio and Fright Talk podcasts. Jones is an Associate Professor at Broward College where he teaches English composition, creative writing, and literature courses. He is a native of Miami, Florida.

Jen Karetnick is an award-winning poet and writer. Based in Miami, she is the author/co-author of 21 books, 11 of which are poetry. Her poems, essays, and articles are published widely. Her widely-acclaimed poetry collection "Inheritance with a High

Error Rate" received the 2022 "Cider Press Review" Book Award.

Steve Kronen: Poems from his three collections have appeared in The American Scholar, The Paris Review, The Southern Review, The Yale Review, Poetry, Plume, and APR. Awards include an NEA; three Florida Individual Artist fellowships; PSA's Hemley Award; Shenandoah's Boatwright Prize; and Sewanee, and Bread Loaf fellowships. He lives with his wife novelist Ivonne Lamazares in Miami.

Mort Laitner is Florida's Jewish short-story writer. Mort has authored, "A Hebraic Obsession", "The Hanukkah Bunny" and "The Greatest Gift." He has produced an award-winning short film entitled, "The Stairs". ChatGPT has said, Mort's works often explore themes of love, loss, and the human connection. His writing style is characterized by its emotional depth and introspection. Laitner's works have garnered praise for their heartfelt expression and keen insight into the human experience.

Mario (Mark) Lew is an author, editor, and alpha-reader whose published short story, Nowhere To Hide, was nominated for a Pushcart Prize in 2022. After 20 years as a construction superintendent building new structures, Mark now uses his skills to build new worlds in the speculative fiction arena. His love of language (and cooking skills) has enabled him to develop delicious metaphor and imagery that leaves most readers happy to eat at his table.

Cathy Lowen is a retired designer, resides in Washington State and loves to travel with her equally retired husband. She has yet to visit the moon…but it's on the list.

Carolyn McBride is the author of The Cicada Spring and Santa Overboard, the first two novels in the Potomac Shores series. Carolyn writes about the places she lives and loves, from South Florida waters to the Occoquan River, through the eyes of a female boat captain. She is a graduate of the College of William and Mary and former editor and columnist for National Geographic Traveler.

Beverly Melasi-Haag truly believes that "Reading is Magic!" She's been a children's reading and writing advocate/author of mystery, how-to, and goal-setting books for over 40 years. Her synergy helps inspire and strengthen children's literacy through reading and creative writing courses, building a community of advocates and educators who can help students improve their skills for the rest of their lives.

Pat B. Milone trained horses, counseled teens, studied fine art, sold her ceramics through Miami art galleries, and coordinated mental health care prior to retiring in Redland farm area, S.W. of Miami. Her poems, haiku and memoir vignettes have been published in Women Moving Forward Vol.3, Multiculti-Mixterations, 45 Literary Magazine, Cadence anthologies, and Miami Poets Soiree anthology.

Joanne Sherry Mitchel: Author of contemporary poetry books that reflect the poet's life experience and wisdom. Her poems are also replete with humor, angst, pragmatism, spirituality, love and hope, most people think and feel but do not express. Her growing up in a family of eight siblings in New York City, experience as a mother, wife, teacher, counselor, and successful Miami real estate business are woven into poetic nuggets of insight for coping with life's challenges.

Anita Mitchell has written, "God took my arms, but he gave me THIS Gift." *The story of Abbas Karimi PLY.* As a child, Abbas began swimming in the Kabul River in Kabul Afghanistan, became a US citizen in 2022 and is on the US Paralympic team in the Paris 2024 Paralympic Games. The book tells how he did it, who helped him along the way and the challenges of his higher calling. For 26 years, Anita worked as an assignment editor/field producer for WSVN-7 Miami.

Keiana Morgan loves creating art. She enjoys designing jewelry,. clothing, and accessories. Keiana gains her inspiration from her family and close friends who motivate and encourage her to create a new piece of art daily.

Christina Moss Mayo writes a column about volunteers for The Miami Herald. She advocates for birds and the environment through her work as a Tropical Audubon Ambassador. Christina taught journalism for 15 years, and was a pioneer in digital information access ten years before the World Wide Web was launched. She is a graduate of the University of Florida.

Barbra Nightingale: Her 10th book of poetry, Spells & Other Ways of Flying (Kelsay Books, 2021), was a Distinguished Favorite in the 2022 Independent Press Awards. Her poems have appeared in Journals such as Rattle, Narrative Magazine, Witchery, Florida Review, Kansas Quarterly,BlueLight /RedLight, Kalliope, Many Mountains Moving, and many others. She is a retired but currently back-at-work English professor, and an Associate Editor with the South Florida Poetry Journal.

Meg Nocero, founder of S.H.I.N.E. Networking Inc., is a trial attorney turned TEDx speaker, life purpose coach, and award-winning author of *The Magical Guide to Bliss, Sparkle & Shine and Butterfly Awakens: A Memoir of Transformation Through Grief*. She hosts the podcast *Manifesting with Meg: Conversations with Extraordinary People*. More info at www.megnocero.com.

Cara Nusinov is the acclaimed innovator of "visual poetry" combining verse with three-dimensional artworks. She is the creator of the famed "Polka Dot Poetry Peacock", a stunning traveling monument to the written word. Cara is a columnist, book fair co-chair, Poetry Therapy Practitioner, and co-creator of the "The Poetry Buffet Party".

Samuel Peralta, PhD, is a physicist, founder, storyteller. Samuel Peralta has designed nuclear robotic tools, built solar plants, and founded companies in optoelectronics, mobile software, sustainable energy, and more.

His poetry has been spotlighted by the *BBC*, the *UK Poetry Society*, the *League of Canadian Poets*, and *Best American Poetry*, and has won numerous awards, including the *Palanca Memorial Award for Literature*. He's the creator and series editor of the *Future Chronicles* anthologies, all of which were #1 bestsellers on *Amazon*, and his own fiction has hit the *USA Today* and *Wall Street Journal* bestsellers lists, and been shortlisted for *Best American Science Fiction & Fantasy*.

He has produced and supported over 120 independent films, including *The Fencer*, which garnered a *Golden Globe* nomination, and *Real Artists*, which won an *Emmy Award*. And he is the founder of the *Lunar Codex* project, sending the works of 35000+ writers, artists, musicians, and filmmakers - from 254 countries, territories, and Indigenous nations - from Earth to space, the Moon, and beyond.

Mikaelo Perez is a Cuban-American writer and visual artist. He worked as a project manager for Verbal Visuals, a series of poem submissions placed in areas of commute, in a collaboration with O, Miami. He works and studies in Florida.

Geoffrey Philp, a Silver Musgrave Medal recipient from the Institute of Jamaica, is the author of "My Name is Marcus," the only graphic novel about the life and legacy of Marcus Garvey, Jamaica's first National Hero. Philp's poem, "A Prayer for My Children," is featured on The Poetry Rail--an homage to 12 writers who shaped Miami's culture. He lives in Miami and is working on a book-length poem, "Letter from Marcus Garvey."

Jonathan Rose is an immigration attorney and a cultural activist. He has served as a judge of local, regional, national, and international poetry contests. An award-winning poet, he has translated poetry, presented poetry workshops, and was nominated for a Pushcart Prize. He received a Shining Star Award "in recognition of extraordinary work . . . whose leadership skills enhance the quality of life in Greater Miami through the arts." He serves as Program Director for the South Florida Writers Association.

Peter Schmitt is the author of six collections of poems, most recently Goodbye, Apostrophe (Regal House). He has also edited, and written the introduction for his late father's Pan Am Ferry Tales: A World War II Aviation Memoir (McFarland). He is a native Miamian.

Brian Shaer is a South Florida-based author and actor. He has degrees in both communications and cinema studies and has presented research on cinema at several academic conferences. His first book, "Are We Living in a Disaster Movie? How Genre

Conventions Predict the Plot of the COVID-19 Pandemic," is available at most online retailers.

C.V. Shaw is a novelist native to South Florida. She is the author behind *"The Spell."* Shaw is a Doctor of Oriental Medicine, a Quantum Energy Medicine Practitioner, and a MindScape Instructor. Shaw's poetry and short stories have been published in several journals. Previously as a journalist, she was a feature writer for *M.D. News, Florida Medical Business, Miami Herald Neighbors* and *Club Systems International.*

Gail Tucker-Griffith, an award-winning internationally published scientist, also earned local and national awards as a science teacher in Miami. Now in her third vocation, she has several awards for memoir, short story and poetry pieces and self-published two children's picture books (#3 is in progress). She shares life with husband Robert, stepdaughter Julie and family, and Sassy Cat Dancer.

Cynthia Uzzolino, a NYC native and mother of 3, began writing poetry at 11 years old. Upon relocating to Florida, she has immersed herself in the local writing community and is currently focused on completing her first novel, and book of poems. Cynthia also volunteers at an elementary school aftercare program, where she mentors children in the art of creative writing.

Dale Alan Young is a Board-Certified Healthcare Chaplain. He is a father and husband with 3 children and 6 grandchildren. His life theme is Borrowed Space, Just Passing Through.

Printed in the USA
CPSIA information can be obtained
at www.ICGtesting.com
CBHW041917051124
16951CB00025B/875